CONTENTS

PEACE CORPS/ZAMBIA
HISTORY AND PROGRAMS

History of the Peace Corps in Zambia

Following the formalization of a country agreement in 1993, Peace Corps/Zambia opened its program in 1994 with a group of water and sanitation/hygiene education Volunteers. In 1996, the program expanded to include projects in community health and rural aquaculture. The program expanded again in 2001 to encompass an income, food, and environment project. In 2003, a new education project was launched. Using emergency HIV/AIDS funding, a separate HIV/AIDS project was launched in 2005. Currently, Peace Corps/Zambia has four projects: rural aquaculture promotion (RAP), rural education development (RED), linking income food and the environment (LIFE), and the community health improvement project (CHIP).

In April 2004, the Peace Corps celebrated its 10th anniversary of service in Zambia. Since the first Peace Corps Volunteers arrived in 1994, approximately 1,280 Volunteers have served in Zambia, which is now one of the largest Peace Corps programs in Africa. Volunteers live and work in eight of the nine provinces of Zambia.

History and Future of Peace Corps Programming in Zambia

Rural Aquaculture Promotion (RAP) Project
Volunteers are helping the Department of Fisheries to develop fish-farming projects that will improve livelihoods in rural communities. After determining rural farmers' needs and resources, Volunteers provide technical assistance in establishing dams, furrows, fishponds, and integrated agriculture. In addition to providing an excellent source of nutrition for rural families, surplus fish and agricultural products are sold to provide substantial supplementary income. Volunteers provide training in small agribusiness skills to assist farmers in applying a business orientation toward their farming activities. Volunteers also help build the organizational development capacity of fish-farming associations.

Linking Income Food and Environment (LIFE) Project
In 2004, the Forestry Department invited Peace Corps/Zambia to partner with it to provide extension services at the community level. The Zambian Forestry Department has no extension officers at the community level (Frontline extension officers). PC/Z is collaborating with the Departments of Forestry to address the issue of conserving the natural resources through promotion of agroforestry, soil conservation and management, improved gardening techniques, and teaching of basic business skills.

Volunteers work together with Department of Forestry staff and lead farmers to develop capacity at the household level. Volunteer activities address food insecurity and livelihood diversification of these communities, thus reducing pressure on forest habitat and natural resources.

Rural Education Development (RED) Project
The RED project now focuses on teaching English as a foreign language (TEFL). The project typically seeks to improve counterpart English proficiency, teaching skills, and participation in professional development, which leads to improved English language instruction and increased communicative English proficiency for students. RED Volunteers teach English to sixth- through eighth-grade students. In addition to TEFL, RED Volunteers may also participate in various informal English instruction activities, such as English camps and clubs and adult TEFL

education, as well as general education activities such as library development and community support groups for schools. Volunteers will receive extensive training to learn how they can use their native English speaker skills to be more aware of language and use that knowledge to support both counterpart teachers and students.

Rural Health Project

In the fall of 2008, Peace Corps/Zambia combined the Community Action for Health project (CAHP) and the HIV/AIDS Project (HAP) to form a new comprehensive rural health project. The project, delivered at the district and community levels, focuses on improving rural health in the areas of malaria, food security, and HIV/AIDS awareness, education, prevention, and nutrition. This is in addition to other health priorities identified by communities in which Volunteers serve. In this rural-based project Volunteers work to facilitate the formation and training of community-based organizations that spearhead the planning, implementation, and sustainable management of community-led intervention in malaria, food security, HIV/AIDS mitigation and management and other community-identified health priorities. The project is implemented under the Ministry of Health and, therefore, the primary contact for the Volunteer is the Rural Health Center and its staff. Volunteers also work with other line ministries and sector organizations to mobilize resources for the training and implementation of sustainable health interventions in the above-stated health areas.

COUNTRY OVERVIEW: ZAMBIA AT A GLANCE

History

Zambia was relatively untouched by the outside world until the mid-19th century, when it was visited by Western explorers, missionaries, and traders. In 1855, David Livingstone became the first European to see the magnificent waterfalls on the Zambezi River. Known locally as *Musi-o-tunya*, or the "Smoke that Thunders," Livingstone renamed the falls after Queen Victoria. The Zambian town near the falls is named after him, and served as the capital of what was called Northern Rhodesia until 1935. In 1888, Northern and Southern Rhodesia (now Zambia and Zimbabwe, respectively) were proclaimed a British sphere of influence. Southern Rhodesia was annexed formally and granted self-government in 1923, while the administration of Northern Rhodesia was transferred to the British colonial office in 1924 as a protectorate. In 1953, both Rhodesias were joined by Nyasaland (now Malawi) to form the Federation of Rhodesia and Nyasaland.

The Republic of Zambia gained its independence from Britain on October 24, 1964. Kenneth Kaunda, the leader of the United National Independence Party, was named the first president and remained in power until 1991. After nearly three decades of one-party rule and worsening economic conditions, the Kaunda era came to an end. In November 1991, the Movement for Multiparty Democracy (MMD) won Zambia's first free presidential and general elections since 1968. Frederick Chiluba was subsequently sworn in as the nation's second president and was re-elected in 1996. In 2002, Levy Mwanawasa was elected president under the banner of the MMD. He was re-elected in 2006, but died of a heart attack in August of 2008. He was succeeded by Rupiah Banda. He served until September 2011 when Patriotic Front (PF) candidate Michael Sata was elected as president.

Historically, copper has provided the majority of the country's foreign exchange earnings and been the leading source of employment. However, the drastic decline in copper market values, a slow rate of industrialization, and a high dependence on foreign imports drove Zambia's economy into an extended decline. Through the early-1990s, Zambia experienced one of the worst economic growth rates in the world. In an effort to halt two decades of economic decline, the country undertook an ambitious economic recovery program. A cornerstone of this program has been the privatization of parastatal industries (including copper mines). However, the nation's extremely high rate of HIV/AIDS infection, along with an unstable food supply and drought, continues to hamper development efforts. Recently, however, copper prices have drastically improved and the mining sector has resumed its position as the No.1 income generator for the country. The government has continued to promote and support the agriculture sector, which is the mainstay of most rural Zambians.

Government

Zambia gained its independence on October 24, 1964. There are three branches of government: the Executive branch, which consists of the president and the cabinet; the Legislative branch, which consists of a unicameral National Assembly; and the Judicial branch, which includes the Supreme Court, high court, lands tribunal, industrial relations court, subordinate courts, small claims court, and local courts. Currently, the ruling political party is the Patriotic Front (PF).

Economy

Zambia is one of sub-Saharan Africa's most highly urbanized countries. Approximately half of the country's nearly 13 million people are concentrated in a few urban zones strung along the major transportation corridors. Unemployment and underemployment are serious problems. Compared to other African countries, Zambia has a relatively low per capita income at $1,461 U.S. (2010). It has a mixed economy with an urban public sector dominated by government, nonprofit nongovernmental organizations (NGOs), and parastatal organizations (many of which have been privatized or are being privatized), and a predominately private rural agricultural sector. Maize (corn) is the principal cash crop and is a staple. There have been positive macroeconomics results, with a decline in the inflation rate to 6.8 percent and an appreciation of the kwacha to U.S. dollar exchange rates.

People and Culture

Zambia is divided into nine provinces and 72 districts. There are 73 ethno-linguistic groups, the predominant ones being Nyanja, Tonga, Lozi, Bemba, Luvale, Kaonde, and Lunda. English is the official language throughout the country; however, in rural areas, it is common to find those who do not speak English. Most Zambians are Christians, and they belong to a wide variety of denominations. Other major religions include Hinduism, Islam, and indigenous beliefs. Ninety-nine percent of the population consists of Black Africans, the rest being European, Asian, and mixed origin. Zambia's life expectancy is 52.36 years. Approximately 14.3 percent of Zambians are infected with HIV, and over 800,000 Zambian children have lost one or both of their parents to HIV/AIDS.

Zambians are very welcoming, open, and friendly people with interesting and diverse cultures and traditions. That said, one of the challenges of finding your place as a Volunteer is fitting into the local culture while maintaining your own cultural identity and professionalism. As a guest in Zambia, you will be expected to respect culture and traditions, and to tolerate or adapt to differences you may encounter. Cultural adaptation is a great opportunity and a rewarding experience.

Environment

Named after the Zambezi River, Zambia is a landlocked country in central southern Africa, and it is surrounded by Angola, Botswana, Malawi, Mozambique, Namibia, Tanzania, Zaire, and Zimbabwe. It is roughly the size of Texas and covers 2.3 percent of Africa's total area. Much of Zambia lies on a plateau with an average height between 3,500 and 4,500 feet (1,066 to 1,371 meters). The huge valleys of the upper Zambezi and its major tributaries, including the Kafue and Luangwa rivers, cut into this plateau. The climate consists of three distinct seasons: a warm, wet season from November to April; a cool, dry season from May to August; and a hot, dry season in September and October. The relatively high altitude tempers the humidity, providing a generally pleasant climate. The diversity of climatic conditions also allows for the cultivation of a wide range of crops.

RESOURCES FOR FURTHER INFORMATION

Following is a list of websites for additional information about the Peace Corps and Zambia and to connect you to returned Volunteers and other invitees. Please keep in mind that although we try to make sure all these links are active and current, we cannot guarantee it. If you do not have access to the Internet, visit your local library. Libraries offer free Internet usage and often let you print information to take home.

A note of caution: As you surf the Internet, be aware that you may find bulletin boards and chat rooms in which people are free to express opinions about the Peace Corps based on their own experience, including comments by those who were unhappy with their choice to serve in the Peace Corps. These opinions are not those of the Peace Corps or the U.S. government, and we hope you will keep in mind that no two people experience their service in the same way.

General Information About Zambia

www.countrywatch.com/
On this site, you can learn anything from what time it is in the capital of Zambia to how to convert from the dollar to the Zambian Kwacha. Just click on Zambia and go from there.

www.lonelyplanet.com/destinations
Visit this site for general travel advice about almost any country in the world.

www.state.gov
The State Department's website issues background notes periodically about countries around the world. Find Botswana and learn more about its social and political history. You can also go to the site's international travel section to check on conditions that may affect your safety.

www.psr.keele.ac.uk/official.htm
This includes links to all the official sites for governments worldwide.

www.geography.about.com/library/maps/blindex.htm
This online world atlas includes maps and geographical information, and each country page contains links to other sites, such as the Library of Congress, that contain comprehensive historical, social, and political background.

www.cyberschoolbus.un.org/infonation/info.asp
This United Nations site allows you to search for statistical information for member states of the U.N.

www.worldinformation.com
This site provides an additional source of current and historical information about countries around the world.

Connect With Returned Volunteers and Other Invitees

www.rpcv.org
This is the site of the National Peace Corps Association, made up of returned Volunteers. On this site you can find links to all the Web pages of the "Friends of" groups for most countries of service, comprised of former Volunteers who served in those countries. There are also regional groups that frequently get together for social events and local volunteer activities.

www.PeaceCorpsWorldwide.org
This site is hosted by a group of returned Volunteer writers. It is a monthly online publication of essays and Volunteer accounts of their Peace Corps service.

Online Articles/Current News Sites About Zambia

http://www.times.co.zm
Times of Zambia

http://www.zambia.co.zm
Zambia Online

http://www.thezambian.com
The Zambian

http://www.postzambia.com
The Post

International Development Sites About Zambia

http://www.usaid.gov/locations/sub-saharan_africa/index.html
USAID's work in sub-Saharan Africa

www.fews.net
USAID Famine Early Warning Systems Network

http://www.worldbank.org
World Bank

Recommended Books

1. Baylies, Carolyn L. and Janet Bujra. *AIDS, Sexuality and Gender in Africa: The Struggle Continues.* Routledge Publishers, 2001.

2. Bull, Schuyler and Alan Male. *Along the Luangwa: The Story of an African Floodplain (Nature Conservancy Habitat).* Soundprints, 1999.

3. Burdette, Marcia. *Zambia: Between Two Worlds.* Boulder, Colo.: Westview Press, 1988.

4. Hansen, Karen Tranberg. *Salaula: The World of Secondhand Clothing and Zambia.* Chicago: University of Chicago Press, August 2000.

5. Kelly, Robert C. (editor), et al. *Zambia Country Review.* CountryWatch.com, December 1999.

6. Swiller, Josh. *The Unheard: A Story of Deafness in Africa.* New York, N.Y.: Henry Holt and Company, 2007

Books About the History of the Peace Corps

1. Hoffman, Elizabeth Cobbs. *All You Need is Love: The Peace Corps and the Spirit of the 1960s*. Cambridge, Mass.: Harvard University Press, 2000.

2. Rice, Gerald T. *The Bold Experiment: JFK's Peace Corps*. Notre Dame, Ind.: University of Notre Dame Press, 1985.

3. Stossel, Scott. *Sarge: The Life and Times of Sargent Shriver*. Washington, D.C.: Smithsonian Institution Press, 2004.

4. Meisler, Stanley. *When the World Calls: The Inside Story of the Peace Corps and its First 50 Years*. Boston, Mass.: Beacon Press, 2011.

Books on the Volunteer Experience

1. Dirlam, Sharon. *Beyond Siberia: Two Years in a Forgotten Place*. Santa Barbara, Calif.: McSeas Books, 2004.

2. Casebolt, Marjorie DeMoss. *Margarita: A Guatemalan Peace Corps Experience*. Gig Harbor, Wash.: Red Apple Publishing, 2000.

3. Erdman, Sarah. *Nine Hills to Nambonkaha: Two Years in the Heart of an African Village*. New York, N.Y.: Picador, 2003.

4. Hessler, Peter. *River Town: Two Years on the Yangtze*. New York, N.Y.: Perennial, 2001.

5. Kennedy, Geraldine ed. *From the Center of the Earth: Stories out of the Peace Corps*. Santa Monica, Calif.: Clover Park Press, 1991.

6. Thompsen, Moritz. *Living Poor: A Peace Corps Chronicle*. Seattle, Wash.: University of Washington Press, 1997 (reprint).

LIVING CONDITIONS AND VOLUNTEER LIFESTYLE

Communications

Mail

Few countries in the world offer the level of service we consider normal in the U.S. If you expect U.S. standards for mail service, you will be in for frustration. Mail takes a minimum of two to four weeks to arrive in Lusaka. Surface mail may take up to five months to be delivered and is highly unlikely to be insurable. Duty fees must be paid on all packages received; the amount depends on the value (or perceived value) of the contents. Though not frequent, some mail may simply not arrive. We recognize that when we are thousands of miles from our families and friends, communication becomes a very sensitive issue. Advise your family and friends to number their letters and to write "Air Mail" and "*Par Avion*" on their envelopes.

Despite delays, we strongly encourage you to write to your family regularly, perhaps weekly or biweekly. Family members will typically become worried when they do not hear from you, so please advise your parents, friends, and relatives that mail is sporadic and that they shouldn't worry if they don't receive your letters regularly.

As a trainee, you will receive mail at the training center near Lusaka.

Your address during training will be:

(Your Name)/PCT
Peace Corps
P.O. Box 50707
Lusaka, Zambia

Telephones

In recent years, Zambia has drastically improved its cellular telephone network and offers a choice between three cellphone companies: Zamtel, MTN, and Celtel. Though coverage in some areas is spotty outside of Lusaka and the provincial capitals, it is available in 75 percent of the districts. The cellphone network has improved over time. Thus, trainees are advised to bring money with them to buy a cell phone soon after arriving in-country. Text messaging is one of the cheapest, most reliable ways to communicate with fellow Volunteers and staff, as well as with friends and family back home.

Computer, Internet, and Email Access

There are several Internet service providers in Zambia. The number of Internet cafes around the country is also growing. The cost of access varies, but tends to be relatively expensive. Due to the nature and quality of the landline connections, all companies offer both digital and analog dial-up numbers.

Computer and email access are available at the provincial houses, though occasionally do not work due to infrastructure or power issues. Internet access is also available and free at the Volunteer resource library in the Peace Corps office in Lusaka. You should prepare yourself and your friends and family to expect limited access to email. Your main sources of communication with family and friends will be via text messaging and handwritten letters.

Due to the lack of electricity and potential for theft, very few Volunteers keep laptop computers at their sites. As Peace Corps has installed wireless Internet in each of the provincial offices/resource centers, many Volunteers have found it very beneficial to bring a netbook or laptop to Zambia. However, if you do bring a laptop, make sure to insure it.

Housing and Site Location

Most Volunteers live in earthen houses lighted by kerosene lamps. Meals are cooked over wood or charcoal. Typically, Volunteer sites are in villages where there is neither plumbing nor electricity. You will have your own mud brick/thatch roof house, pit latrine, outdoor cooking area, and shower area. Drinking/washing water may need to be carried from as far as 30 minutes away by foot. Some sites will be very isolated and the closest Volunteer may be 40 kilometers or more away. A select number of Volunteers may live in these same conditions, but within 5 kilometers of a small town center.

Within the first week of arriving in Zambia, you will be assigned the language you will be speaking. The associate Peace Corps director (APCD) of your program may offer advice based on the various skills and interest of individuals in your group. Your final placements are made in cooperation with the training staff and are based on their assessments and recommendations regarding your skill levels in the technical, cross-cultural, and language areas. PC medical staff members are also consulted on your site placement to ensure your medical concerns do not worsen. Your APCD can discuss particular preferences concerning a site. *You will not be able to choose your site.* Site placements are made using the following criteria (in priority order):

- Medical considerations

- Community needs

- Site requirements matched with demonstrated technical, cross cultural, and language skills

- Personal preference of the Volunteer

Living Allowance and Money Management

The local currency is the Zambian kwacha (Zkw). Since 2010, the value of the kwacha has remained around 5,000 Zkw per one U.S. dollar.

As a Volunteer in Zambia you will receive five types of allowances: a living allowance, vacation allowance, travel allowance, settling-in allowance, and readjustment allowance.

The living allowance covers your basic living expenses. It is reviewed at least once per year through a market survey to ensure that it is adequate. In Zambia, this is typically $200 to $300 each month and is paid in local currency. This allowance is disbursed to Volunteers through locally established personal bank accounts on a quarterly basis. It is intended to cover expenses, including food, household supplies, clothing, recreation, transportation, reading materials, and other incidentals. By comparison, your local Zambian peers working for the government will be making about $250 a month.

A standard Peace Corps vacation allowance amounting to $24 a month will be added to your living allowance. This is also paid on a quarterly basis in local currency.

A travel allowance is paid to you on a quarterly basis, together with your living allowance. This allowance is to cover all planned events, such as travel to in-service training, provincial meetings, mid-term medicals, and the close-of-service conference. When on official Peace Corps/Zambia travel, you will be given additional money for transportation and meals.

A one-time settling-in allowance, also paid in ZKw at an equivalency of roughly $290, is given to buy basic household items when you move to your site. In addition, a security upgrade fund, equivalent to $35, is added to be used for Volunteers' homes.

A readjustment allowance of $275 is accumulated each month. One-third is given to you prior to your departure and the balance is sent to your home of record after you return.

Due to the potential for theft, we advise that you not bring more than $250 if you do bring cash for travel and vacation. Traveler's checks are becoming harder to cash. Some foreign exchange posts do not accept $1 or $5 bills, and you will receive a lower exchange rate for $10 and $20 notes. If you plan to travel outside of Zambia on vacation, some U.S. currency may be needed for airport fees, visas, and other expenses, which must be paid in U.S. dollars. We suggest bringing an ATM card and credit card for emergencies or travel, as well. Cashing personal checks or checks that family or friends may want to send is extremely complicated and should be avoided. Instead, family or friends can deposit money directly into your U.S. bank account. Peace Corps/Zambia cannot facilitate any personal banking.

Food and Diet

Your access to Western-style foods may be very limited, but you will soon become familiar, and even enamored with, *nshima* (cornmeal porridge), cabbage, and *kapenta* (fish), as well as other staple foods like local leaf sauces and smoked fish. Fruits such as mangoes, guavas, and especially bananas, can be found everywhere, but mangoes are seasonal; vegetable variety is generally good, but can be seasonally difficult; and meat is not readily available for Volunteers while at their sites.

Ideally, mealtime should be a time of relaxation, but, in an unfamiliar country, mealtimes will, at first, be an unsettling challenge. The available food may seem strange in type and appearance; it may even initially appear unpalatable. Yet, you may feel obligated to demonstrate your friendliness and willingness to accept local customs by eating food that doesn't appeal to you. You'll need to stay within your comfort zone, but remember that the local cuisine, customs, and expectations are very different from your own. If you are not prepared to make some major adjustments in your lifestyle, you will very likely experience a great deal of frustration.

During pre-service training, you will have many opportunities to become familiar with what is available, as well as how to prepare and cook a wide variety of foods. Some Volunteers can gain weight due to the carbohydrate-based diet.

Volunteer Comment:

> *"I have had no trouble whatsoever being a vegetarian. The Peace Corps staff was very helpful and accommodating during training—they went out of their way to explain to the host families of the vegetarians about our diets. Zambians have been really understanding as well. There are times when meat is prepared for special occasions, and guests of honor are sometimes given the gizzard of a chicken to eat, but I haven't had any trouble with politely declining meat. Food access varies depending on where you're posted in the country, but I haven't had any trouble maintaining a healthy diet, free of meat."*

Transportation

All Volunteers will be expected to travel in Zambia using local means of transportation like your Zambian peers (foot, bicycle, bus, van, or train) from your first days of training until the end of your service. Rural travel is very limited and difficult due to the condition of the roads and public transportation. Every trip is an adventure. Transportation from your post to your provincial capital may be sporadic, may take a full day or more, and will generally be crowded and dusty. It may take two days or more by crowded public transportation to reach the capital city, Lusaka. Some Volunteers walk or ride their bikes up to 50 kilometers (31 miles) or more to catch a ride at a main road. Some roads are not easily passable by bicycle in the rainy season. All Volunteers will be provided with a bicycle and helmet, which they must wear when riding. Riding motorcycles is prohibited.

Geography and Climate

Zambia is a landlocked country positioned in southern Africa and is bordered by the countries of Botswana, Angola, Namibia, D.R.O.C., Tanzania, Malawi, Mozambique, and Zimbabwe. It is located south of the Equator and is in both the eastern and southern hemispheres.

Most of the country consists of a wide plateau with some scattered mountains. Though located in the tropical latitudes, the general height of the land gives Zambia a more pleasant climate with relatively low humidity. There are three seasons—cool and dry from May to August, hot and dry from September to November, and warm and wet from December to April. Only in the valleys of the Zambezi and Luangwa is there excessive heat.

Social Activities

Social activities will vary depending on where you are located. These may include taking part in various festivities, parties, storytelling, and sitting around a fire at night talking with your neighbors. Some Volunteers visit nearby Volunteers on weekends and make occasional trips to their provincial capital, although we encourage Volunteers to remain at their sites to accomplish the important Peace Corps goal of cultural exchange.

Professionalism, Dress, and Behavior

One of the challenges of finding your place as a Volunteer is simultaneously fitting into the local culture, maintaining your own cultural identity, and acting like a professional. It is not an easy act to balance, and we can only provide you with some guidelines to dress and behave accordingly. While some of your counterparts may dress in seemingly worn or shabby clothes, this will be due to economics rather than choice. The likelihood is that they are wearing their "best." A foreigner wearing raggedy, unkempt clothing is more likely to be considered an affront.

Zambians regard dress and appearance as part of one's respect for one another. They value neatness of appearance, which is much more important than being "stylish." You are expected to dress appropriately, whether you are in training, traveling, or on the job. Not doing so may jeopardize your credibility and that of the entire program.

Dress guidelines have been formalized based not only on advice from Zambians, but also on the experiences of current Volunteers. Dresses and skirts should fall below the knees. Appropriate undergarments should be worn, including slips. Spaghetti tops for women worn by themselves are inappropriate unless covered with a short- or long-sleeved/shirt, coat or jacket. Skin-tight sports shorts or trousers are inappropriate but may be worn under a skirt or dress when riding bicycles. Men and women should wear shorts only at home, when exercising, or when doing work where Zambian counterparts are also wearing them. If shorts are worn in public, they should be of "walking" length. Hair should be clean and combed, and beards should be neatly trimmed. Men should never wear a hat indoors unless custom in the area allows, and they should always be removed when speaking to an elder. Sunglasses should also be removed when indoors.

PC training staff will send you back to your homestay to dress appropriately if you come to class in what they will consider culturally or professionally inappropriate dressings.Long hair on men, unconventional hairdos, blatant tattoos, and facial piercings are not culturally appropriate and may negatively affect community integration. Facial piercings are considered inappropriate and should not be worn during Volunteer service. Tattoos should be covered with clothing. If you have any of these appearance characteristics, a decision to go without them for the duration of your Peace Corps service should be made prior to accepting the invitation to serve in Zambia.

Personal Safety

More detailed information about the Peace Corps' approach to safety is contained in the "Health Care and Safety" chapter, but it is an important issue and cannot be overemphasized. As stated in the Volunteer Handbook, becoming a Peace Corps Volunteer entails certain safety risks. Living and traveling in an unfamiliar environment (oftentimes alone), having a limited understanding of local language and culture, and being perceived as well-off are some of the factors that can put a Volunteer at risk. Many Volunteers experience varying degrees of unwanted attention and harassment. Petty thefts and burglaries are not uncommon, and incidents of physical and sexual assault do occur, although most Zambia Volunteers complete their two years of service without incident. The Peace Corps has established procedures and policies designed to help you reduce your risks and enhance your safety and security. These procedures and policies, in addition to safety training, will be provided once you arrive in Country X. Using these tools, you are expected to take responsibility for your safety and well-being.

Each staff member at the Peace Corps is committed to providing Volunteers with the support they need to successfully meet the challenges they will face to have a safe, healthy, and productive service. We encourage Volunteers and families to look at our safety and security information on the Peace Corps website at www.peacecorps.gov/safety.

Information on these pages gives messages on Volunteer health and Volunteer safety. There is a section titled "Safety and Security —Our Partnership." Among topics addressed are the risks of serving as a Volunteer, posts' safety support systems, and emergency planning and communications.

Rewards and Frustrations

The excitement and adventure of the Volunteer experience are, in some measure, due to its unpredictability. There will be unexpected joys, as well as unexpected disappointments. You could find plans for a health clinic canceled at the last minute because the Ministry of Health has been reorganized. Your plan to dig a well may be held up by a quarrel between local groups over who is to do the digging or because the required materials cannot be delivered as scheduled. The official to whom you were supposed to report may be replaced by a successor who knows little about a scheduled project. Such variables can erode the enthusiasm, patience, and idealism of a Volunteer. Your success will often depend upon determination, patience, and the ability to find another way. A Peace Corps Volunteer always has to be able to come up with a Plan B and many times, a Plan C, D, or even E! A big part of the Peace Corps is the challenge to remain flexible, energetic, and hopeful at a time when it would be easy to give in to cynicism or indifference. Accepting the community and being accepted by it is essential for success. In both your daily life and in your work, Volunteers must take care to avoid the appearance of superiority or arrogance that can be associated with an outsider bringing "change" and "improvements." Volunteers find that as they live and work in their communities, they learn as much or more from the people of their host countries than they share in return.

PEACE CORPS TRAINING

Pre-Service Training

Pre-service training is the most intensive period of your Peace Corps service. During your nine weeks of training time, you will need to accumulate the knowledge and experience necessary for the first several months of service. Before being sworn in as a Volunteer, you will also need to demonstrate that you meet the criteria to qualify for Volunteer service.

Following a brief orientation program, you will be taken to a current Volunteer's site to spend a few days observing firsthand what the next two years have in store for you. Following this first site visit, you will proceed to one of two Peace Corps training centers where you will live with a host family. While pre-service training is extremely busy, it is also a time of excitement, discovery, and self-fulfillment. Drawing on your reserves of patience and humor, the effort and frustrations of functioning in a different culture will be rewarded with a sense of belonging among new friends. The long hours of study and practice will pay off in your ability to work effectively in a challenging job that will directly benefit a great number of people.

Trainees in all program sectors will follow a community-based training model. You will live with homestay families in villages within 15-20 kilometers of the training center. Your language, cross-culture, and technical sessions will take place in surrounding villages. At least once a week, you will travel by bike to the training center for medical and other sessions and travel back to your homestay family at the end of the day. The living situation with your families will be similar to what you will experience as a Volunteer.

Technical Training

Technical training will prepare you to work in Zambia by building on the skills you already have and helping you develop new skills in a manner appropriate to the needs of the country. The Peace Corps staff, Zambia experts, and current Volunteers will conduct the training program. Training places great emphasis on learning how to transfer the skills you have to the community in which you will serve as a Volunteer.

Technical training will include sessions on the general economic and political environment in Zambia and strategies for working within such a framework. You will review your technical sector's goals and will meet with the Zambian agencies and organizations that invited the Peace Corps to assist them. You will be supported and evaluated throughout the training to build the confidence and skills you need to undertake your project activities and be a productive member of your community.

Language Training

As a Peace Corps Volunteer, you will find that language skills are key to personal and professional satisfaction during your service. These skills are critical to your job performance, they help you integrate into your community, and they can ease your personal adaptation to the new surroundings. Therefore, language training is at the heart of the training program. You must successfully meet minimum language requirements to complete training and become a Volunteer. Zambian language instructors teach formal language classes five days a week in small groups of four to five people.

Your language training will incorporate a community-based approach. In addition to classroom time, you will be given assignments to work on outside of the classroom and with your host family. The goal is to get you to a point of basic social communication skills so you can practice and develop language skills further once you are at your site. Prior to being sworn in as a Volunteer, you will work on strategies to continue language studies during your service.

Cross-Cultural Training

As part of your pre-service training, you will live with a Zambian host family. This experience is designed to ease your transition to life at your site. Families go through an orientation conducted by Peace Corps staff to explain the purpose of pre-service training and to assist them in helping you adapt to living in Zambia. Many Volunteers form strong and lasting friendships with their host families.

Cross-cultural and community development training will help you improve your communication skills and understand your role as a facilitator of development. You will be exposed to topics such as community mobilization, conflict resolution, gender and development, nonformal and adult education strategies, and political structures.

Health Training

During pre-service training, you will be given basic medical training and information. You will be expected to practice preventive health care and to take responsibility for your own health by adhering to all medical policies. Trainees are required to attend all medical sessions. The topics include preventive health measures and minor and major medical issues that you might encounter while in Zambia. Nutrition, mental health, setting up a safe living compound, and how to avoid HIV/AIDS and other sexually transmitted diseases (STDs) are also covered.

Safety Training

During the safety training sessions, you will learn how to adopt a lifestyle that reduces your risks at home, at work, and during your travels. You will also learn appropriate, effective strategies for coping with unwanted attention and about your individual responsibility for promoting safety throughout your service.

Additional Trainings During Volunteer Service

In its commitment to institutionalize quality training, the Peace Corps has implemented a training system that provides Volunteers with continual opportunities to examine their commitment to Peace Corps service while increasing their technical and cross-cultural skills. During service, there are usually three training events. The titles and objectives for those trainings are as follows:

- In-service training: *Provides an opportunity for Volunteers to upgrade their technical, language, and project development skills while sharing their experiences and reaffirming their commitment after having served for three to six months.*

- Midterm conference (done in conjunction with technical sector in-service): *Assists Volunteers in reviewing their first year, reassessing their personal and project objectives, and planning for their second year of service.*

- Close-of-service conference: *Prepares Volunteers for the future after Peace Corps service and reviews their respective projects and personal experiences.*

The number, length, and design of these trainings are adapted to country-specific needs and conditions. The key to the training system is that training events are integrated and interrelated, from the pre-departure orientation through the end of your service, and are planned, implemented, and evaluated cooperatively by the training staff, Peace Corps staff, and Volunteers.

YOUR HEALTH CARE AND
SAFETY IN ZAMBIA

The Peace Corps' highest priority is maintaining the good health and safety of every Volunteer. Peace Corps medical programs emphasize the preventive, rather than the curative, approach to disease. The Peace Corps in Zambia maintains a clinic with a full-time medical officer, who takes care of Volunteers' primary health care needs. Additional medical services, such as testing and basic treatment, are also available in Zambia at local hospitals. If you become seriously ill, you will be transported either to an American-standard medical facility in the region or to the United States.

Health Issues in Zambia

Zambia is a very healthy country to live in, provided you use your common sense and pay particular attention to situations that could easily be prevented. Commonly encountered health problems here are colds, coughs, flu, strep throat, diarrhea, skin infections and fevers. Depending on your immunization history, you will receive immunizations against rabies, hepatitis A and B, meningococcal meningitis, and typhoid.

One significant illness you could be exposed to is *Plasmodium falciparum* malaria. During pre-service training, you will be fully informed about its life cycle, the steps you need to take to prevent getting it, how to diagnose it, what to do for self-treatment, and when you should contact the medical officer. Malaria can be a fatal disease, so we take it very seriously. Taking malaria prophylaxis is not a negotiable issue; Volunteers are expected to take it as prescribed, and failure to do this could result in administrative separation. Mefloquine is the main anti-malarial taken by Volunteers. For those who do not tolerate it, doxycycline (taken daily) is an alternative. Malarone will be given only if you cannot tolerate mefloquine or doxycycline. The Peace Corps, in conjunction with the Centers for Disease Control and Prevention, has determined that mefloquine is the preferred malaria prophylaxis in chloroquine-resistant areas; and given data collected from the many Volunteers who have taken it for two years or more, it has been deemed very safe. If, however, you feel you will NOT want to take mefloquine or any of the other two prophylaxis, you may want to consider going to a nonmalarial country. Remember, noncompliance with your malaria prophylaxis is viewed very seriously.

Nutrition is the cornerstone not only to a healthy body, but also to a healthy service. It is, therefore, imperative that you eat nutritionally. Throughout pre-service training, you will learn
how to maintain a well-balanced diet. Once you get to your site,
you will need to allow yourself the time for "hunting and gathering." Changing your mindset from a fast food culture to one in which significant time and energy must be expended can be challenging. However, this can be done in ways that will allow you to also develop and secure your status as a respected and valued member of your community and village.

Zambia currently has one of the highest incidences of HIV/AIDS in Africa. In a country with a population of 10 million, the Zambia Ministry of Health reports that an estimated 950,000 adults and 70,000 children are currently infected with the HIV virus. Approximately 16 percent of men and women between the ages of 15 and 49 are HIV positive. More than 75 percent of Zambian AIDS cases come from sexually active young adults and children under 5 who were infected by their mothers at birth. The country is experiencing an alarming rise in the number of children left orphaned because of AIDS. The effect of HIV/AIDS on Zambia is widespread, affecting not only the family structure, but also the country's economy and education system. The disease will continue to adversely affect the country's already low life expectancy.

Your health in Zambia should not be an issue if you make sensible, healthy choices.

Helping You Stay Healthy

The Peace Corps will provide you with all the necessary inoculations, medications, and information to stay healthy. Upon your arrival in Zambia, you will receive a medical handbook. At the end of training, you will receive a medical kit with supplies to take care of mild illnesses and first aid needs. The contents of the kit are listed later in this chapter.

During pre-service training, you will have access to basic medical supplies through the medical officer. However, you will be responsible for your own supply of prescription drugs and any other specific medical supplies you require, as the Peace Corps will not order these items during training. Please bring a three-month supply of any prescription drugs you use, since they may not be available here and it may take several months for shipments to arrive.

You will have physicals at midservice and at the end of your service. If you develop a serious medical problem during your service, the medical officer in Zambia will consult with the Office of Medical Services in Washington, D.C. If it is determined that your condition cannot be treated in Zambia, you may be sent out of the country for further evaluation and care.

Maintaining Your Health

As a Volunteer, you must accept considerable responsibility for your own health. Proper precautions will significantly reduce your risk of serious illness or injury. The adage "An ounce of prevention …" becomes extremely important in areas where diagnostic and treatment facilities are not up to the standards of the United States. The most important of your responsibilities in Zambia is to take the following preventive measures:

Many illnesses that afflict Volunteers worldwide are entirely preventable if proper food and water precautions are taken. These illnesses include food poisoning, parasitic infections, hepatitis A, dysentery, Guinea worms, tapeworms, and typhoid fever. Your medical officer will discuss specific standards for water and food preparation in Zambia during pre-service training.

Abstinence is the only certain choice for preventing infection with HIV and other sexually transmitted diseases. You are taking risks if you choose to be sexually active. To lessen risk, use a condom every time you have sex. Whether your partner is a host country citizen, a fellow Volunteer, or anyone else, do not assume this person is free of HIV/AIDS or other STDs. You will receive more information from the medical officer about this important issue.

Volunteers are expected to adhere to an effective means of birth control to prevent an unplanned pregnancy. Your medical officer can help you decide on the most appropriate method to suit your individual needs. Contraceptive methods are available without charge from the medical officer.

It is critical to your health that you promptly report to the medical office or other designated facility for scheduled immunizations, and that you let the medical officer know immediately of significant illnesses and injuries.

Women's Health Information

Pregnancy is treated in the same manner as other Volunteer health conditions that require medical attention but also have programmatic ramifications. The Peace Corps is responsible for determining the medical risk and the availability of appropriate medical care if the Volunteer remains in-country. Given the circumstances under which Volunteers live and work in Peace Corps countries, it is rare that the Peace Corps' medical and programmatic standards for continued service during pregnancy can be met.

If feminine hygiene products are not available for you to purchase on the local market, the Peace Corps medical officer in Zambia will provide them. If you require a specific product, please bring a three-month supply with you.

Your Peace Corps Medical Kit

The Peace Corps medical officer will provide you with a kit that contains basic items necessary to prevent and treat illnesses that may occur during service. Kit items can be periodically restocked at the medical office.

Medical Kit Contents

Ace bandages

Adhesive tape

American Red Cross First Aid & Safety Handbook

Antacid tablets (Tums)

Antibiotic ointment (Bacitracin/Neomycin/Polymycin B)

Antiseptic antimicrobial skin cleaner (Hibiclens)

Band-Aids

Butterfly closures

Calamine lotion

Cepacol lozenges

Condoms

Dental floss

Diphenhydramine HCL 25 mg (Benadryl)

Insect repellent stick (Cutter's)

Iodine tablets (for water purification)

Lip balm (Chapstick)

Oral rehydration salts

Oral thermometer (Fahrenheit)

Pseudoephedrine HCL 30 mg (Sudafed)

Robitussin-DM lozenges (for cough)

Scissors

Sterile gauze pads

Tetrahydrozaline eyedrops (Visine)

Tinactin (antifungal cream)

Tweezers

Before You Leave: A Medical Checklist

If there has been any change in your health—physical, mental, or dental—since you submitted your examination reports to the Peace Corps, you must immediately notify the Office of Medical Services. Failure to disclose new illnesses, injuries, allergies, or pregnancy can endanger your health and may jeopardize your eligibility to serve.

If your dental exam was done more than a year ago, or if your physical exam is more than two years old, contact the Office of Medical Services to find out whether you need to update your records. If your dentist or Peace Corps dental consultant has recommended that you undergo dental treatment or repair, you must complete that work and make sure your dentist sends requested confirmation reports or X-rays to the Office of Medical Services.

If you wish to avoid having duplicate vaccinations, contact your physician's office to obtain a copy of your immunization record and bring it to your pre-departure orientation. If you have any immunizations prior to Peace Corps service, the Peace Corps cannot reimburse you for the cost. The Peace Corps will provide all the immunizations necessary for your overseas assignment, either at your pre-departure orientation or shortly after you arrive in Zambia. You do not need to begin taking malaria medication prior to departure.

Bring a three-month supply of any prescription or over-the-counter medication you use on a regular basis, including birth control pills. Although the Peace Corps cannot reimburse you for this three-month supply, it will order refills during your service. While awaiting shipment—which can take several months—you will be dependent on your own medication supply. The Peace Corps will not pay for herbal or nonprescribed medications, such as St. John's wort, glucosamine, selenium, or antioxidant supplements.

You are encouraged to bring copies of medical prescriptions signed by your physician. This is not a requirement, but they might come in handy if you are questioned in transit about carrying a three-month supply of prescription drugs.

If you wear eyeglasses, bring two pairs with you—a pair and a spare. If a pair breaks, the Peace Corps will replace them, using the information your doctor in the United States provided on the eyeglasses form during your examination. The Peace Corps discourages you from using contact lenses during your service to reduce your risk of developing a serious infection or other eye disease. Most Peace Corps countries do not have appropriate water and sanitation to support eye care with the use of contact lenses. The Peace Corps will not supply or replace contact lenses or associated solutions unless an ophthalmologist has recommended their use for a specific medical condition and the Peace Corps' Office of Medical Services has given approval.

If you are eligible for Medicare, are over 50 years of age, or have a health condition that may restrict your future participation in health care plans, you may wish to consult an insurance specialist about unique coverage needs before your departure. The Peace Corps will provide all necessary health care from the time you leave for your pre-departure orientation until you complete your service. When you finish, you will be entitled to the post-service health care benefits described in the Peace Corps *Volunteer Handbook*. You may wish to consider keeping an existing health plan in effect during your service if you think age or pre-existing conditions might prevent you from re-enrolling in your current plan when you return home.

Safety and Security—Our Partnership

Serving as a Volunteer overseas entails certain safety and security risks. Living and traveling in an unfamiliar environment, a limited understanding of the local language and culture, and the perception of being a wealthy American are some of the factors that can put a Volunteer at risk. Property theft and burglaries are not uncommon. Incidents of physical and sexual assault do occur, although almost all Volunteers complete their two years of service without serious personal safety problems.

Beyond knowing that Peace Corps approaches safety and security as a partnership with you, it might be helpful to see how this partnership works. Peace Corps has policies, procedures, and training in place to promote your safety. We depend on you to follow those policies and to put into practice what you have learned. An example of how this works in practice—in this case to help manage the risk of burglary—is:

- Peace Corps assesses the security environment where you will live and work

- Peace Corps inspects the house where you will live according to established security criteria

- Peace Corps provides you with resources to take measures such as installing new locks

- Peace Corps ensures you are welcomed by host country authorities in your new community

- Peace Corps responds to security concerns that you raise

- You lock your doors and windows

- You adopt a lifestyle appropriate to the community where you live

- You get to know neighbors

- You decide if purchasing personal articles insurance is appropriate for you

- You don't change residences before being authorized by Peace Corps

- You communicate concerns that you have to Peace Corps staff

Factors that Contribute to Volunteer Risk

There are several factors that can heighten a Volunteer's risk, many of which are within the Volunteer's control. By far the most common crime that Volunteers experience is theft. Thefts often occur when Volunteers are away from their sites, in crowded locations (such as markets or on public transportation), and when leaving items unattended.

Before you depart for Zambia there are several measures you can take to reduce your risk:

- Leave valuable objects in the U.S.

- Leave copies of important documents and account numbers with someone you trust in the U.S.

- Purchase a hidden money pouch or "dummy" wallet as a decoy

- Purchase personal articles insurance

After you arrive in Zambia, you will receive more detailed information about common crimes, factors that contribute to Volunteer risk, and local strategies to reduce that risk. For example, Volunteers in Zambia learn to:

- Choose safe routes and times for travel, and travel with someone trusted by the community whenever possible

- Make sure one's personal appearance is respectful of local customs

- Avoid high-crime areas

- Know the local language to get help in an emergency

- Make friends with local people who are respected in the community

- Limit alcohol consumption

As you can see from this list, you must be willing to work hard and adapt your lifestyle to minimize the potential for being a target for crime. As with anywhere in the world, crime does exist in Zambia. You can reduce your risk by avoiding situations that place you at risk and by taking precautions. Crime at the village or town level is less frequent than in the large cities; people know each other and generally are less likely to steal from their neighbors. Tourist attractions in large towns are favorite worksites for pickpockets. While whistles and exclamations may be fairly common on the street, this behavior can be reduced if you dress conservatively, abide by local cultural norms, and respond according to the training you will receive.

Staying Safe: Don't Be a Target for Crime

You must be prepared to take on a large degree of responsibility for your own safety. You can make yourself less of a target, ensure that your home is secure, and develop relationships in your community that will make you an unlikely victim of crime. While the factors that contribute to your risk in Zambia may be different, in many ways you can do what you would do if you moved to a new city anywhere: Be cautious, check things out, ask questions, learn about your neighborhood, know where the more risky locations are, use common sense, and be aware. You can reduce your vulnerability to crime by integrating into your community, learning the local language, acting responsibly, and abiding by Peace Corps policies and procedures. Serving safely and effectively in Zambia will require that you accept some restrictions on your current lifestyle.

Support from Staff

If a trainee or Volunteer is the victim of a safety incident, Peace Corps staff is prepared to provide support. All Peace Corps posts have procedures in place to respond to incidents of crime committed against Volunteers. The first priority for all posts in the aftermath of an incident is to ensure the Volunteer is safe and receiving medical treatment as needed. After assuring the safety of the Volunteer, Peace Corps staff response may include reassessing the Volunteer's worksite and housing arrangements and making any adjustments, as needed. In some cases, the nature of the incident may necessitate a site or housing transfer. Peace Corps staff will also assist Volunteers with preserving their rights to pursue legal sanctions against the perpetrators of the crime. It is very important that Volunteers report incidents as they occur, not only to protect their peer Volunteers, but also to preserve the future right to prosecute. Should Volunteers decide later in the process that they want to proceed with the prosecution of their assailant, this option may no longer exist if the evidence of the event has not been preserved at the time of the incident.

Crime Data for Zambia

Crime data and statistics for Zambia, which are updated yearly, are available at the following link: http://www.peacecorps.gov/countrydata/zambia Please take the time to review this important information.

Few Peace Corps Volunteers are victims of serious crimes, and crimes that do occur overseas are investigated and prosecuted by local authorities through the local courts system. If you are the victim of a crime, you will decide if you wish to pursue prosecution. If you decide to prosecute, Peace Corps will be there to assist you. One of our tasks is to ensure you are fully informed of your options and understand how the local legal process works. Peace Corps will help you ensure your rights are protected to the fullest extent possible under the laws of the country.

If you are the victim of a serious crime, you will learn how to get to a safe location as quickly as possible and contact your Peace Corps office. It's important that you notify Peace Corps as soon as you can so Peace Corps can provide you with the help you need.

Volunteer Safety Support in Zambia

The Peace Corps' approach to safety is a five-pronged plan to help you stay safe during your service and includes the following: information sharing, Volunteer training, site selection criteria, a detailed emergency action plan, and protocols for addressing safety and security incidents. Zambia's in-country safety program is outlined below.

The Peace Corps/Zambia's office will keep you informed of any issues that may impact Volunteer safety through **information sharing**. Regular updates will be provided in Volunteer newsletters and in memorandums from the country director. In the event of a critical situation or emergency, you will be contacted through the emergency communication network. An important component of the capacity of Peace Corps to keep you informed is your buy-in to the partnership concept with the Peace Corps staff. It is expected that you will do your part in ensuring that Peace Corps staff members are kept apprised of your movements in-country so they are able to inform you.

Volunteer training will include sessions on specific safety and security issues in Zambia. This training will prepare you to adopt a culturally appropriate lifestyle and exercise judgment that promotes safety and reduces risk in your home, at work, and while traveling. Safety training is offered throughout service and is integrated into the language, cross-cultural aspects, health, and other components of training. You will be expected to successfully complete all training competencies in a variety of areas, including safety and security, as a condition of service.

Certain **site selection criteria** are used to determine safe housing for Volunteers before their arrival. The Peace Corps staff works closely with host communities and counterpart agencies to help prepare them for a Volunteer's arrival and to establish expectations of their respective roles in supporting the Volunteer. Each site is inspected before the Volunteer's arrival to ensure placement in appropriate, safe, and secure housing and worksites. Site selection is based, in part, on any relevant site history; access to medical, banking, postal, and other essential services; availability of communications, transportation, and markets; different housing options and living arrangements; and other Volunteer support needs.

You will also learn about Peace Corps/Zambia's **detailed emergency action plan,** which is implemented in the event of civil or political unrest or a natural disaster. When you arrive at your site, you will complete and submit a site locator form with your address, contact information, and a map to your house. If there is a security threat, you will gather with other Volunteers in Zambia at predetermined locations until the situation is resolved or the Peace Corps decides to evacuate.

Finally, in order for the Peace Corps to be fully responsive to the needs of Volunteers, it is imperative that Volunteers immediately report any security incident to the Peace Corps office. The Peace Corps has established **protocols for addressing safety and security incidents** in a timely and appropriate manner, and it collects and evaluates safety and security data to track trends and develop strategies to minimize risks to future Volunteers.

DIVERSITY AND
CROSS-CULTURAL ISSUES

In fulfilling its mandate to share the face of America with host countries, the Peace Corps is making special efforts to assure that all of America's richness is reflected in the Volunteer corps. More Americans of color are serving in today's Peace Corps than at any time in recent history. Differences in race, ethnic background, age, religion, and sexual orientation are expected and welcomed among our Volunteers. Part of the Peace Corps' mission is to help dispel any notion that Americans are all of one origin or race and to establish that each of us is as thoroughly American as the other despite our many differences.

Our diversity helps us accomplish that goal. In other ways, however, it poses challenges. In Zambia, as in other Peace Corps host countries, Volunteers' behavior, lifestyle, background, and beliefs are judged in a cultural context very different from their own. Certain personal perspectives or characteristics commonly accepted in the United States may be quite uncommon, unacceptable, or even repressed in Zambia.

Outside of Zambia's capital, residents of rural communities have had relatively little direct exposure to other cultures, races, religions, and lifestyles. What people view as typical American behavior or norms may be a misconception, such as the belief that all Americans are rich and have blond hair and blue eyes. The people of Zambia are justly known for their generous hospitality to foreigners; however, members of the community in which you will live may display a range of reactions to cultural differences that you present.

To ease the transition and adapt to life in Zambia, you may need to make some temporary, yet fundamental compromises in how you present yourself as an American and as an individual. For example, female trainees and Volunteers may not be able to exercise the independence available to them in the United States; political discussions need to be handled with great care; and some of your personal beliefs may best remain undisclosed. You will need to develop techniques and personal strategies for coping with these and other limitations. The Peace Corps staff will lead diversity and sensitivity discussions during pre-service training and will be on call to provide support, but the challenge ultimately will be your own.

Overview of Diversity in Zambia

The Peace Corps staff in Zambia recognizes the adjustment issues that come with diversity and will endeavor to provide support and guidance. During pre-service training, several sessions will be held to discuss diversity and coping mechanisms. We look forward to having male and female Volunteers from a variety of races, ethnic groups, ages, religions, and sexual orientations, and hope that you will become part of a diverse group of Americans who take pride in supporting one another and demonstrating the richness of American culture.

What Might a Volunteer Face?

Possible Issues for Female Volunteers

Zambia is a paternalistic society. Young female Volunteers may experience some frustration when Zambian men do not take them seriously at first or view them as children. Female Volunteers may also receive more unwanted and inappropriate attention from Zambian men. They may have to work harder than male Volunteers to gain the respect of colleagues in the workplace. They may not be accorded the respect they are normally accustomed to receiving.

Volunteer Comment:

"Being a female Volunteer in Zambia isn't always easy. Concepts of 'gender equality' and 'sexual harassment' aren't what they are in the States. Work situations can be difficult, particularly if you are young, because you often find yourself working with men who aren't used to taking women as seriously as you are probably accustomed to. You may find yourself plagued with marriage proposals, questions about boyfriends, or inquires about your cooking abilities, rather than questions related to work. Despite these challenges, it is possible to develop great friendships with men here and show the men that you know and work with that women are capable of much more than they might have thought."

Possible Issues for Volunteers of Color

In Zambian cities and towns, it is fair to say that most Zambians are aware of some of the different racial and ethnic groups that exist in the United States. However, among rural populations, this level of knowledge and understanding greatly diminishes.

African Americans may not be recognized as Americans and may be asked what their tribal language and customs are. They may be expected to learn local languages more quickly than other Volunteers. They may be accepted more readily into the culture than other Volunteers or treated according to local social norms because it is assumed they are African. They may not be recognized as Americans or may be perceived as considering themselves superior to Africans. They may be discriminated against by white Africans.

Hispanic American Volunteers may also be perceived as not being American; they may be labeled as Cubans or Mexicans. Zambians may expect Hispanics to automatically assume different role patterns or to interact socially with more ease. Asian-American Volunteers may be subject to stereotypes based on behavior Zambians have observed in films, such as being assumed to be experts at kung fu, and based on Zambia's current or historical involvement with Asian countries. They also may not be seen as American.

Volunteer Comment:

"As a Volunteer of color, I have really enjoyed my experience. However, there are challenges here that may have never occurred to you. Constantly being asked where you are from and then being told that you can't be an American because Americans are white, does get tiring after a while. There is also the 'Muzungu factor.' You may be told that muzungu *means white person, and then promptly afterwards you will have small children running after you screaming* muzungu. *I get called* muzungu *all of the time. They know that I am not white, but they also see that I am not Zambian. What I have done to combat this is to ensure that, at least where I live, everyone calls me by name, and if someone from another area happens to be visiting and calls me* muzungu, *they are corrected by my friends, neighbors, and work partners. Don't let this get to you; it is just another aspect of life here. Also, rap music and martial arts movies are popular here, so be prepared for some assumptions based on stereotypes and being greeted in terms that you might find offensive. Finally, you can find support from fellow Volunteers and staff, so please do come and join us. It is well worth it."*

Possible Issues for Senior Volunteers

In Zambia, older members of society are viewed and treated with a great deal of respect. Issues for older Americans are more likely to be in relation to their younger fellow Peace Corps Volunteers. Older Volunteers may work and live with individuals in the Peace Corps community who have little understanding of, or respect for, the lives and experiences of senior Americans. Senior Volunteers may not get necessary personal support from younger Volunteers and may be reluctant to share personal, sexual, or health concerns with them or with members of the Peace Corps staff. They may find that younger Volunteers look to them for advice and support; a role they may not enjoy assuming. During pre-service training, senior Volunteers may need to be assertive when developing an effective approach to language learning.

Volunteer Comment:

"The village life here is rigorous, with lots of bike riding and fairly harsh living conditions. Being, on average, 20 to 30 years older than the next Volunteer can get tiresome sometimes. Also, you have to determine your place in your training group and in the larger Volunteer community. If you want to be seen in a surrogate parent/grandparent role or if you do not, it is up to you to establish those parameters. Some Volunteer activities you will want to be left out of; others you won't. Be vocal and let other Volunteers know what you do like to do so they will include you. I've found that many assumptions are made based on age in the Peace Corps and Zambian communities. The respect that you will receive because of a few gray hairs is, I must admit, quite nice, but being left out of something because they figure you wouldn't be interested is annoying, but can be avoided. Language learning is the biggest challenge here. If you have never learned one before, once you've figured it out,

you will need to explain to the training staff your learning style. Ask for extra instruction, study, and practice speaking as much as you can! It does make a difference."

Possible Issues for Married Couple Volunteers

Married couples may face the challenge of one spouse being more enthusiastic about the Peace Corps, one spouse being better able to adapt to the new environment, or one spouse being less or more homesick than the other. A married man may be encouraged by Zambians to be the more dominant member in the relationship, to make decisions independent of his wife's views, or to socialize without his wife. He may be ridiculed if he performs domestic tasks or refuses to have a mistress. A married woman may find herself in a less independent role than she is accustomed to. She may have a more limited social life in the community than single female Volunteers because of Zambians' assumption that she is busy taking care of her husband. She may be expected to perform more domestic chores than her husband.

Volunteer Comment:

"My husband and I are agriculture/environment Volunteers in the southern province. As a married couple, we benefit from the convenience of processing our daily experience together, an elevated status in the village, and of having someone to take care of you when you've got a bout of horrendous diarrhea. The challenging part has been finding answers to questions and statements such as: 'Why don't you have children?' 'Why is your husband cooking? That's your role.' 'Does your husband beat you?' and 'Why do you wear pants? Women are supposed to wear chitenges.*' The way you choose to answer these questions is entirely personal and may change over time. People here are sincerely curious about American ways, and I remind myself daily the cross-cultural experience goes both ways. Although your experience as a married couple, and as individuals, may be challenging, it will also be exciting, fun, rewarding, and provide a new opportunity for relationship development. Even in the short time we have been here, people are starting to accept (maybe not understand) that my husband and I are equals in our relationship. We do equal housework, and we are both here to work with the community. This experience has given our relationship a deeper level of trust and confidence. It has provided us the opportunity to become truly comfortable with who we are in the face of hard questions and cultural differences."*

Possible Issues for Gay, Lesbian, or Bisexual Volunteers

In general, Zambians view homosexuality as immoral and as something that has been "imported" from Europe. Homosexual activity is against the law in Zambia and although few cases are brought before the courts, it still requires that homosexuals be mindful that anti-gay laws and sentiment exist. While there are certainly homosexuals, the level of tolerance will probably not be what it was in the States. Due to cultural norms, homosexual Volunteers may discover they cannot be open about their sexual preference in their communities. Volunteers may serve for two years without meeting another gay Volunteer. Lesbians will have to deal with constant questions about boyfriends, marriage, and sex (as do all women). Most Zambian homosexuals have probably migrated to the larger cities, while most Volunteers are posted in rural sites. Gay men must deal with machismo: talk of conquest(s), girl watching, and dirty jokes.

Volunteer Comment:

"Homosexual activity is illegal here, and generally not spoken about, nor widely recognized. Depending on where you come from in the U.S., the level of tolerance here probably won't be what you're used to back home. Zambians will often ask you about your fiancé/husband/wife/girlfriend/boyfriend, and as other Volunteers come from a range of backgrounds, you'll find within them a range of levels of support/acceptance/etc. Although being gay here presents unique difficulties, keep in mind that: a) It is possible to find support (there's a diversity committee made up of

Volunteers and staff) and find love(!); and b) this experience, as a whole, is incredible and, I think, worth whatever difficulties you face as an 'un-heterosexual.' Everyone faces their own challenges here, even if they're not gay!"

A recommended resource for support and advice prior to and during your service is the Lesbian, Gay, Bisexual & Transgender U.S. Peace Corps Alumni website at **www.lgbrpcv.org**.

Possible Religious Issues for Volunteers

Zambia is a declared Christian nation; most Zambians have some religious affiliation and attend church regularly. Zambia has a wide variety of Christian faiths, a very small number of Muslims (mainly in the Asian community), and a few other religions, such as Hindu and B'hai. In Zambia, the questions, "Are you a Christian?" and "Do you pray?" are conversation starters. Volunteers may be chastised for not observing Christian beliefs or asked to explain why they don't practice a certain Christian denomination. They may be expected to attend church with their communities or they may be actively recruited by a Christian group. Volunteers may have difficulty conveying their beliefs due to language and cultural barriers.

Volunteer Comment:

"Religion is an important part of the culture in Zambia, and I am often asked which church I belong to. I never went to church back home, but I thought I would go at least once during my service. It was a long service, and as it was in the local language and I understood very little. However, it was an enjoyable experience, as there was a great deal of singing and dancing. Zambians are very loud, joyful, and outspoken during church service, and that is easy to appreciate, regardless of which language you speak."

Possible Issues for Volunteers With Disabilities

As part of the medical clearance process, the Peace Corps Office of Medical Services determined that you were physically and emotionally capable, with or without reasonable accommodations, to perform a full tour of Volunteer service in Country X without unreasonable risk of harm to yourself or interruption of service. The Peace Corps/ Country X staff will work with disabled Volunteers to make reasonable accommodations for them in training, housing, jobsites, or other areas to enable them to serve safely and effectively.

FREQUENTLY ASKED QUESTIONS

How much luggage am I allowed to bring to Zambia?
Most airlines have baggage size and weight limits and assess charges for transport of baggage that exceeds those limits. The Peace Corps has its own size and weight limits and will not pay the cost of transport for baggage that exceeds these limits. The Peace Corps' allowance is two checked pieces of luggage with combined dimensions of both pieces not to exceed 107 inches (length + width + height) and a carry-on bag with dimensions of no more than 45 inches. Checked baggage should not exceed 100 pounds total with a maximum weight of 50 pounds for any one bag.

Peace Corps Volunteers are not allowed to take pets, weapons, explosives, radio transmitters (shortwave radios are permitted), automobiles, or motorcycles to their overseas assignments. Do not pack flammable materials or liquids such as lighter fluid, cleaning solvents, hair spray, or aerosol containers. This is an important safety precaution.

What is the electric current in Zambia?
The local current is 220 to 240 volts, 50 cycles. You will need a transformer to use American appliances here. There are also power surge fluctuations and outages that take a toll on equipment. A solar battery recharger may be useful, and a solar charger for your electronics is recommended.

In general, most Volunteers do not recommend bringing electrical appliances because 95 percent of Volunteers do not have electricity at their sites. The exceptions are Volunteer leaders in the provincial capital and a few Lusaka-based Volunteers.

How much money should I bring?
Volunteers are expected to live at the same level as the people in their community. You will be given a settling-in allowance and a monthly living allowance, which should cover your expenses. Volunteers often wish to bring additional money for vacation travel to other countries. Credit cards and traveler's checks are preferable to cash. If you choose to bring extra money, bring the amount that will suit your own travel plans and needs.

When can I take vacation and have people visit me?
Each Volunteer accrues two vacation days per month of service (excluding training). Leave may not be taken during training, the first three months of service, or the last three months of service, except in conjunction with an authorized emergency leave. Family and friends are welcome to visit you after pre-service training and the first three months of service as long as their stay does not interfere with your work. Extended stays at your site are not encouraged and may require permission from your country director. The Peace Corps is not able to provide your visitors with visa, medical, or travel assistance.

Will my belongings be covered by insurance?
The Peace Corps does not provide insurance coverage for personal effects; Volunteers are ultimately responsible for the safekeeping of their personal belongings. However, you can purchase personal property insurance before you leave. If you wish, you may contact your own insurance company; additionally, insurance application forms will be provided, and we encourage you to consider them carefully. Volunteers should not ship or take valuable items overseas. Jewelry, watches, radios, cameras, and expensive appliances are subject to loss, theft, and breakage, and in many places, satisfactory maintenance and repair services are not available.

Do I need an international driver's license?
Volunteers in Zambia do not need an international driver's license because they are prohibited from operating privately owned motorized vehicles. Most urban travel is by bus or taxi. Rural travel ranges from buses and minibuses to trucks, bicycles, and lots of walking. On very rare occasions, a Volunteer may be asked to drive a sponsor's vehicle, but this can occur only with prior written permission from the country director. Should this occur, the Volunteer may obtain a local driver's license. A U.S. driver's license will facilitate the process, so bring it with you just in case.

What should I bring as gifts for Zambia friends and my host family?

This is not a requirement. A token of friendship is sufficient. Some gift suggestions include knickknacks for the house; pictures, books, or calendars of American scenes; souvenirs from your area; hard candies that will not melt or spoil; or photos to give away.

Where will my site assignment be when I finish training and how isolated will I be?

Peace Corps trainees are not assigned to individual sites until after they have completed pre-service training. This gives Peace Corps staff the opportunity to assess each trainee's technical and language skills prior to assigning sites, in addition to finalizing site selections with their ministry counterparts. If feasible, you may have the opportunity to provide input on your site preferences, including geographical location, distance from other Volunteers, and living conditions. However, keep in mind that many factors influence the site selection process and that the Peace Corps cannot guarantee placement where you would ideally like to be. Most Volunteers live in small towns or in rural villages and are usually within one hour from another Volunteer.

How can my family contact me in an emergency?

The Peace Corps' Counseling and Outreach Unit (COU) provides assistance in handling emergencies affecting trainees and Volunteers or their families. Before leaving the United States, instruct your family to notify the Counseling and Outreach Unit immediately if an emergency arises, such as a serious illness or death of a family member. During normal business hours, the number for the Counseling and Outreach Unit is 855.855.1961, then select option 2; or directly at 202-692-1470. After normal business hours and on weekends and holidays, the COU duty officer can be reached at the above number. For non-emergency questions, your family can get information from your country desk staff at the Peace Corps by calling 855.855.1961.

Can I call home from Zambia?

Long-distance telephone communication is available, but it can be difficult at times and it will always be very expensive.Thus, many Volunteers choose to text with their family and friends back home in the States. Calling cards can be used on private phones with the assistance of an operator and the cost will be considerably less. Many Volunteers use this method when they are in Lusaka or in their provincial capitals. Each of the Peace Corps Volunteer leader houses, situated in five provinces, has a phone, so it is possible to arrange a time to receive a phone call. Most post offices in the major cities have international services, but only during their regular hours.

Should I bring a cellular phone with me?

Most cellphones from the U.S. are not adapted for use in Zambia. You can easily buy one here at an affordable price when you arrive. In addition, the cellular service is expensive and, though expanding, remains limited. If you would like to bring a phone from the United States, be sure it is an unlocked quad band, GSM cellphone. Ask the person from whom you are buying the phone whether it can be used in the United Kingdom. If it will work there, it will work here.

Will there be email and Internet access? Should I bring my computer?

Computers and email access are available at each Peace Corps provincial resource center. Each is equipped with wireless Internet in addition to a computer provided by Peace Corps. Therefore, many PCVs choose to come with a laptop/netbook that they can store at the provincial center when they are at home in their village. Internet access in the rural areas is more difficult to find because there are only a few Internet cafes around the country. The cost of accessing the Internet in these cafes varies but tends to be relatively expensive. Internet access is available free of charge in the resource library in the Peace Corps office in Lusaka.

WELCOME LETTERS FROM
ZAMBIA VOLUNTEERS

Dear Peace Corps/Zambia Invitee,

First and foremost—congratulations! Almost three years ago, I received something similar to the very welcome letter you hold in your hands now, inviting me to serve in Peace Corps/Zambia. I ran and grabbed my laptop, Googled "Zambia" and soaked up as much information as I could about the place I would spend the next two (and later it become three) years of my life. I tried to picture my little thatched hut, my neighbors, the rain, the landscape, the future projects I would work on. Looking back now, none of that research and imagining helped a single bit or even came close.

Not that it's going to stop you. However, the most important piece of advice I can give you is to just let it happen; let Zambia seep into your being. Soak up as much as you can while you are here, and forget what you thought you knew about rural Africa, about Zambia, about poverty or development, about the world. Because if you let it, this place will awe you and inspire you and transform you into something you only hinted at before.

Serving as a Volunteer in Zambia is still very much in line with the "traditional" Peace Corps model—following training, you get dropped off at your new rural home, devoid of electricity or running water, with some supplies and little else. Overwhelming? Of course! Rewarding? It is what you make it. You'll eat local foods like *nshima* (Zambia's maize-based staple), *ifisashi* (vegetables cooked in peanut sauce), and dried bean leaves. You'll learn (and struggle through learning) a local language absent anywhere outside of Zambia.

But more than that, you'll serve a country whose people are extremely excited you are coming and who are more welcoming and willing to give than anyone else in the world (but maybe I'm biased, staying an additional year and all). You'll expand your understanding of sub-Saharan Africa exponentially and work on projects that have extreme highs and extreme lows and, throughout the whole process, learn more about yourself and share more about yourself and your own country and culture than maybe you even thought you knew. You'll make relationships that last a lifetime, both with Zambians and Americans and other people you meet along the way, and most of all, you will experience the beautiful tonic of human interconnectedness.

Thinking back to that spring day three years ago, when I held in my hand the letter welcoming me to a country I barely knew anything about but which still managed to shape and mold me into something wholly new, I can't help but be excited for what you're getting ready to do. Congratulations once again, and good luck with the rest of your exciting new journey.

Mukatusanga ('you will find us'),

John Bosco

Incoming Volunteers,

Hey guys! I remember how completely jazzed I was when I received my acceptance letter. I had waited so long for it and it had finally arrived. I immediately Googled Zambia because I had no idea where in Africa it was. I was so excited to be going to Africa, I didn't really care where Zambia was on said continent. I wanted to be placed somewhere completely different than what I was used to. I definitely got my wish. So far I am about one year into my two years of service and I am loving it! It has been amazing so far. Zambia is gorgeous and the people are really friendly. It's not all roses and rainbows and there are certainly a number of challenges, ranging from a completely different culture to missing family, friends, and Mexican food. However, I can wholeheartedly say that I, without reservation, feel very fortunate to be involved in Peace Corps/Zambia.

It seems like forever since I was packing for my two years of service. I really stressed myself out over what to bring. Don't worry, though, everything you need is already here. All you have to do is come. I know I am looking forward to meeting you all. See you soon!

Heather Reinig

Congratulations on being placed in beautiful Zambia—home of *Mosi-oa-Tunya* ("the smoke that thunders") or Victoria Falls, the Zambezi River, Zampop, *nshima,* and the all-purpose *chitenge*. You are about to embark upon a truly life-changing adventure with both its challenges and successes. And you could not have asked to be placed in a better program or country. The cornerstones of Zambian culture rest upon hospitality, friendliness, communal support, and tribal cousinship. These elements, in addition to the lifelong relationships you create during your 27 months here, make Zambia an ideal environment to accomplish the goals of Peace Corps.

In addition to its phenomenal people, Zambia's beauty is supplemented by its natural resources and landscapes. Zambia has a tropical climate with three seasons—hot, rainy, and cold—which varies slightly due to altitude. The landscape throughout the country is absolutely breathtaking, with rolling hills, treed plains, lush vegetation, and vast drylands. Moreover, the stunning horizon of motley sunsets, furious storms, and crystal clear starry nights makes each day indescribable and unique.

Language adds another unique aspect to your service. Of the 73 government-recognized languages throughout the country, Volunteers are taught Bemba, Kaonde, Lunda, Mambwe, Nyanja, or Tonga depending on their provincial placement. Each province—Central, Eastern, Luapula, Lusaka, Northern, Northwestern, and Southern— provides different traditions, natural attractions, languages, weather, and social dynamics, which you will quickly embrace, work within, and call your own.

Being a Peace Corps Volunteer has been described as the "toughest job you'll ever love," but here in Zambia, you could say working it is the "toughest job you'll ever love and share with incredible people." Congratulations again on your placement in Zambia. The experience awaiting you promises to be unlike anything you have ever known.

Mwayaii mwane ("Welcome" in Kaonde),

Audra Blanchfield

Dear African Adventurer,

Congratulations on accepting your invitation to Zambia, one of the last Peace Corps countries in the world that still embodies that original rural spirit of adventure! During our service here, we have experienced some of the greatest challenges and also some of the most rewarding experiences of our lives. Although we do not have actual elephants running through our fields here (goats on the other hand …), we have had the opportunity to accomplish projects neither of us would have ever been able to do in the United States. For myself, a civil engineer and natural resource economist, I have helped my village build a 3-meter high earthen dam to provide water for cows during the dry season. For Rasa, an anthropologist, she has taught the villagers to revamp their traditional use of milk to make cheese for food security and with the dairy cooperative to add value to their products.

You will learn more than you believe your brain can process during training. Before you know it, you will have learned a new language, technical skills, cooking over a wood-fire, mastered bicycling over difficult terrain, and learned how to properly sway your hips to a Zam-pop song. The staff during our pre-service training made sure we learned from our host families how to cope with all the conditions we may encounter during our time in the village. These rustic conditions initially tested us beyond what we thought possible, but with some womanly touches and the help of technology our mud hut is now a very comfortable home. All those tasks that seemed "scary" or foreign at first are now part of our daily routine. We have grown comfortable communicating in our broken but ever improving Tonglish (speaking half Tonga and English). I can now carry 50 liters of water in one go. And Rasa can now make pizza on charcoal, with everything, including the mozzarella cheese, made from scratch in the village.

Faster than you think possible, Zambia will begin to feel like home. Your new village will adopt you wholeheartedly as a member of its family and you will become the next member of our Peace Corps family.

See you soon,

Robert and Rasa Kent

PACKING LIST

This list has been compiled by Volunteers serving in Zambia and is based on their experience. Use it as an informal guide in making your own list, bearing in mind that each experience is individual. There is no perfect list! You obviously cannot bring everything on the list, so consider those items that make the most sense to you personally and professionally. You can always have things sent to you later. As you decide what to bring, keep in mind that you have an 100-pound weight limit on baggage. And remember, you can get almost everything you need in Zambia.

General Clothing

- a good rain jacket

- a fleece or light jacket (it does get cold)

- a couple of long-sleeved shirts

- a sweater

- 3–4 good-quality T-shirts

- 2-year supply of cotton underwear and socks

- 1 bathing suit

- knee-length shorts for sports or wearing around your house

- 2–3 pairs of comfortable pants

- hat (baseball or safari-type to shade you from the sun)

- Women

- lots of bras (especially sports bras)

- 2 nicer tops or blouses (must be modest)

- 2 long easy-care skirts or dresses (must be to the knee)

- Men

- 2 pairs of dressy, easy-care, trousers (khaki is good)

- 2 button-down shirts

- 1 tie

Shoes

- 2 pairs of good sandals (e.g., Tevas or Chacos)

- 1 pair of sneakers

- A pair of shoes that can be worn when trying to look nice

Personal Hygiene and Toiletry Items

Unless you have favorite brands you can't do without, you should be able to buy what you need in Lusaka and provincial capitals. These include cosmetics, soap, toothpaste, general cleaning products and deodorants, hair conditioner, good razors and razor blades, Q-tips, and hair-care products. Bring just enough to get you through training. The Peace Corps provides brand-name tampons; bring only enough for training.

Miscellaneous

- Umbrella

- Headlamp (2)

- Sleeping bag

- Tent

- Leatherman or Swiss Army knife

- Music (iPod)

- Mini-speakers

- Laptop: Please be aware that you will need to store it at the provincial house and that repairs and maintenance will be expensive.

- Solar charger for your iPod and digital camera

- Shortwave radio (3–7 band)

- Games (cards, chess, Scrabble, etc.)

- Hair elastics

- Two sturdy water bottles (e.g., Nalgene)

- Sunglasses (2)

- Camera with memory cards

- Travel alarm clock

- Small backpack/bag

- Money belt

- Journal

- Fitted bed-sheet (full-size)

- Bicycle saddlebags

- 10 or more color photos of you (photo booth-type is OK) for visas, work permits, and ID cards

Optional

- Spices

- Can opener

- Basic cookbook

- Zip-close storage bags

- Packaged mixes for rice, pasta, sauces, and drinks (e.g., Kool Aid, Crystal Light single servings), etc.

- Binoculars

- Small sewing kit

- Pictures or posters for hut decoration

- Bandana

- Duct tape

- Guitar (bring a lot of extra strings and picks)

- Sports equipment (football, volleyball, basketball, Frisbees, etc.)

- Fishing equipment

- Batteries (you can buy them here, but they are expensive)

- Sleeping pad

- U.S. stamps (letters may be mailed in the States by people traveling home from post)

- Maps of the United States and the world (good teaching aids and wall hangings)

- Art supplies, sketch book

- Padded mailing envelopes

- good markers/pens

PRE-DEPARTURE CHECKLIST

The following list consists of suggestions for you to consider as you prepare to live outside the United States for two years. Not all items will be relevant to everyone, and the list does not include everything you should make arrangements for.

Family

- Notify family that they can call the Peace Corps' Counseling and Outreach Unit at any time if there is a critical illness or death of a family member (24-hour telephone number: 1-855-855-1961, then press 2; or directly at 202-692-1470).

- Give the Peace Corps' *On the Home Front* handbook to family and friends.

Passport/Travel

- Forward to the Peace Corps travel office all paperwork for the Peace Corps passport and visas.

- Verify that your luggage meets the size and weight limits for international travel.

- Obtain a personal passport if you plan to travel after your service ends. (Your Peace Corps passport will expire three months after you finish your service, so if you plan to travel longer, you will need a regular passport.)

Medical/Health

- Complete any needed dental and medical work.

- If you wear glasses, bring two pairs.

- Arrange to bring a three-month supply of all medications (including birth control pills) you are currently taking.

Insurance

- Make arrangements to maintain life insurance coverage.

- Arrange to maintain supplemental health coverage while you are away. (Even though the Peace Corps is responsible for your health care during Peace Corps service overseas, it is advisable for people who have pre-existing conditions to arrange for the continuation of their supplemental health coverage. If there is a lapse in coverage, it is often difficult and expensive to be reinstated.)

- Arrange to continue Medicare coverage if applicable.

Personal Papers

- Bring a copy of your certificate of marriage or divorce.

Voting

- Register to vote in the state of your home of record. (Many state universities consider voting and payment of state taxes as evidence of residence in that state.)

- Obtain a voter registration card and take it with you overseas.

- Arrange to have an absentee ballot forwarded to you overseas.

Personal Effects

- Purchase personal property insurance to extend from the time you leave your home for service overseas until the time you complete your service and return to the United States.

Financial Management

- Keep a bank account in your name in the U.S.

- Obtain student loan deferment forms from the lender or loan service.

- Execute a Power of Attorney for the management of your property and business.

- Arrange for deductions from your readjustment allowance to pay alimony, child support, and other debts through the Office of Volunteer Financial Operations at 855.855.1961, extension 1770.

- Place all important papers—mortgages, deeds, stocks, and bonds—in a safe deposit box or with an attorney or other caretaker.

CONTACTING PEACE CORPS HEADQUARTERS

This list of numbers will help connect you with the appropriate office at Peace Corps headquarters to answer various questions. You can use the toll-free number and extension or dial directly using the local numbers provided. Be sure to leave the toll-free number and extensions with your family so they can contact you in the event of an emergency.

Peace Corps Headquarters Toll-free Number: 855.855.1961, Press 1 or the Ext. # (see below)

Peace Corps' Mailing Address: Peace Corps Headquarters
1111 20th Street, NW
Washington, DC 20526

For Questions About:	Staff:	Toll-Free Ext:	Direct/Local Number:
Responding to an Invitation:	Office of Placement	x1840	202.692.1840
Country Information:	Angela Glenn	x2316	202.692.2316
	Desk Officer / Zambia and Botswana		
	zambia@peacecorps.gov		
Plane Tickets, Passports, Visas, or other travel matters:			
	CWT SATO Travel	x1170	202.692.1170
Legal Clearance:	Office of Placement	x1840	202.692.1840
Medical Clearance and Forms Processing (includes dental):			
	Screening Nurse	x1500	202.692.1500
Medical Reimbursements (handled by a subcontractor):			800.818.8772
Loan Deferments, Taxes, Financial Operations:		x1770	202.692.1770

Readjustment Allowance Withdrawals, Power of Attorney, Staging (Pre-Departure Orientation), and Reporting Instructions:

Office of Staging	x1865	202.692.1865

Note: You will receive comprehensive information (hotel and flight arrangements) three to five weeks prior to departure. This information is not available sooner.

Family Emergencies (to get information to a Volunteer overseas) *24 hours:*

Counseling &	x1470	202.692.1470
Outreach Unit